train wine
leaf ladybug
wooly worm
necklace key
cricket
star apple

Wish—ing

Shooting Stars, Four——Leaf
Clovers, and Other Wonders to Wish Upon

Compiled by Gloria T. Delamar

RUNNING PRESS
PHILADELPHIA · LONDON

A RUNNING PRESS MINIATURE EDITION™

Copyright © 1996 by Gloria T. Delamar
Illustrations © 1996 Kurt Vargo

Printed in China.

Library of Congress Cataloging-in-Publication Number 95–71976
ISBN 1–56138–717–7

This book may be ordered by mail from the publisher.
Please include $1.00 for postage and handling.
But try your bookstore first!

Running Press Book Publishers
125 South Twenty-second Street
Philadelphia, Pennsylvania 19103–4399

contents

Introduction–7 ⓐ Acorn–11 · Amulet–12

Apple–13 · Automobile–14 ⓑ Barrel–15

Beetle–16 · Birds–17 · Book–20 · Bridge–21

Butterfly–22 ⓒ Cake, Birthday–24 · Cake,

Wedding–25 · Candle–26 · Cattle–28 · Clock–29

Cloud–30 · Clover–32 · Coin–33 · Comb–34

Corn on the Cob–35 · Cricket–36 ⓓ Dande-

lion–38 · Desire–39 · Dew–40 · Dinnerware–41

Dog–42 · Donkey–44 ⓔ Earring–45 · Egg, Laid

on Good Friday–46 · Eyelash–47 $\mathcal{F}$ Feather–50 ·

Fingernails–51 $\mathcal{G}$ Grass–52 $\mathcal{H}$ Halloween–

53 · Hay Wagon–54 · Horse–55 · Horseshoe–56

$\mathcal{I}$ Ides, Wishing on a Day of–58 · Itching–60

$\mathcal{J}$ Jockey–63 · Jug–64 $\mathcal{K}$ Key–65 · Knife–

66 $\mathcal{L}$ Ladder–67 · Ladybug–68 · Leaf–69

Lightning–72 · Lightning Bug–74 $\mathcal{M}$ Mail

Truck–75 · Moon–76 · Mustard Seed–78 $\mathcal{N}$

Necklace–79 · New Year's–80 · Niagara Falls–81

Night, White Rabbit–82 · Nuts–83 $\bigcirc$ Opos-

sum–84 $\mathcal{P}$ Pea Pod–85 · Pin–86 · Potato Chip–

introduction

Make a wish. . . . You've probably wished on birthday candles, wishbones, and the evening star. But do you know how to wish on a clock, an eyelash, a frog, a leaf, or "white rabbit night"?

Here's an A-to-Z directory of more than eighty wishing customs, things to wish on, plus some important taboos. Some wishing customs are ancient, others modern; some are practiced worldwide, others locally—and some by only a few families. This is folklore in its truest sense.

Such traditions quickly cross borders, so identifying the origins of certain wishes is virtually impossible, though an attempt has been made in this book.

Most of these wishing customs were found in folklore books. The more modern or unusual wishes were recounted by friends and family members who hail from all around the world.

Many wishing rituals have more than one version, so feel free to develop your own method. After all, wishing is a highly personal matter.

Scientists speculate that our impulse to make a wish lies in our desire to believe in an interceding power, but most people participate in wishing customs with a combination of skepticism, playfulness, and hope. Even non-superstitious people will admit to making wishes. Why? Because wishing makes us feel good; it makes us feel in control. So even though we may feel doubt, we'll still cross our fingers and sense our spirits rising as we hope that "wishing will make it so."

May all your wishes come true!

acorn

If an acorn falls while you're standing under an oak tree, pick it up, turn around three times, and make a wish. To make the acorn's magic stronger, place it on a windowsill for three days.

This custom probably comes from the old Scandinavian tradition of putting an acorn in the window so that Thor, god of thunder and lightning, would spare the house.

amulet

If you wish to have
safe travel, wear a
silver amulet and
rub it three times as
the journey begins,
while wishing for
safe passage.

apple

If you can slice an
apple into equal
halves without cutting
or nicking a seed,
your wish for
love will come true.

automobile

If you see an automobile with only one of its headlights lit, say "perdiddle" and make a wish as you touch your nose. If others are present, the first one to say "perdiddle" gets to make a wish while tweaking someone else's nose.

barrel

If you find an
empty barrel,
hold both hands
against it as you
make a wish.

beetle

If you see
a beetle fall on
its back, quickly
make a wish.

birds

If you see three birds
perched together on
one wire, make a wish.
If you finish your wish
before any of them
flies away, your wish
will come true.

book

If you accidentally drop
a book, step on it with
one foot and make a
wish. Be sure to pick it
up with the hand that's
opposite the foot you
used; otherwise, your
wish won't come true.

bridge

If you ride over a bridge you've never crossed before, lift your feet off the floor of the vehicle you're riding in and make a wish. (The driver, for obvious reasons, isn't supposed to make a wish.)

Maryland

butterfly

It's a lucky sign for a butterfly to land on you; whatever wish you make will come true—but make your wish before the butterfly disappears from view.

cake, birthday

If you blow out all the candles on your birthday cake with one breath, your wish will be granted—just don't tell anyone what it is.

This is one of the most widely practiced wishing customs in the world.

cake, wedding

When cutting a wedding cake,
the bride and bridegroom should each put
one hand on the knife, and make
silent wishes as they make the first cut.

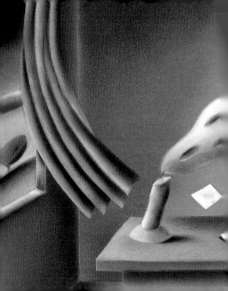

candle

If a candle goes out by
itself before it's burned all
the way down, quickly
make a wish so the spirits
can carry it to the wind.
This is also supposed to
ward off evil spirits.

cattle

If you see cattle
lie down on
Christmas Day,
make a wish.

clock

If you happen to catch
sight of a clock whose two
hands have come together,
quickly make a wish. But
don't watch for it; this will
cancel the clock's magic.

cloud

If you see
a cloud
in the shape
of a camel,
make a wish.

clover

If you find a four-leaf clover, say the following chant while touching each leaf in turn:

"One leaf for fame,
One leaf for wealth,
One for a faithful lover,
One for glorious health;
All in this four-leafed clover."

When you've finished the chant, twirl the clover between two fingers of your right hand and make a wish for one of the four things the clover holds for you.

coin

If you find a coin
(especially a penny),
make a wish on it.
If you spend it,
your wish won't
come true.

comb

If you find a comb
with the teeth pointing
away from you,
make a wish. If the
teeth are pointing
toward you, the comb
isn't "wishable."

corn
on the
cob

If you have an ear
of corn with either
seven or fourteen rows,
make a wish as you
take your first bite.

cricket

A cricket in the house, particularly on the
hearth, brings good luck; so make a wish
on it. If the cricket chirps, there's a better
chance that your wish will come true.

ENGLAND

dandelion

When dandelions have changed to white fluffs, pick one, make a wish, and then blow on the fluff. If you blow off all the fluffs in one breath, some will fly away to grant your wish.

Pennsylvania

desire

If you see someone you
desire, whisper that
person's name twenty
times. Then before going
to sleep that night,
wish twenty times to see
that person again.

UNITED STATES

dew

If you find dew
on a morning
glory, wet your
lips with it and
make a wish.

dinnerware

A diner who is served food in a
dish with a flaw or chip may make a wish
when taking the first bite of food.
(Switching dishes so that you'll get the "wish
dish" will invalidate the wish.)

dog

When you see a dog
chase its tail, quickly
make a wish before it
settles down. If the dog
stops circling before
you finish, your wish
won't come true.

donkey

If you hear a donkey bray, make a wish. If it brays three times, it will help your wish to come true.

earring

If you lose
an earring, make
a wish on the
remaining one.

egg,

Good Friday

Make a wish on an
egg laid on a Good Friday.
A Good Friday egg is
considered a lucky charm that
protects the hen house.

eyelash

If an eyelash accidentally falls out, make a wish on it. This won't work with eyelashes you've pulled out. Put the eyelash on the back of your hand, close your eyes, and gently blow while you make a wish. If the eyelash has blown off your hand, your wish will come true. It's not fair to overdo the blowing.

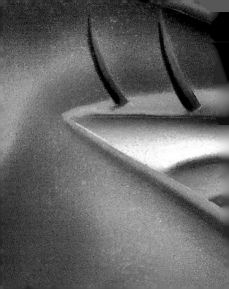

feather

If you find a black feather, stick it in the ground so it stands up, and then make a wish.

If you find a white feather, stick it into the crack of a tree trunk and walk around the tree as you make a wish. As long as the feather stays in the tree trunk there's a chance that your wish will come true.

fingernail

If you discover specks on your fingernails, make a wish and say:

> "Specks on the fingers—
> Fortune lingers;
> Specks on the thumbs—
> Fortune comes."

When you trim your fingernails, make a wish on the cuttings before throwing them away where no one else can get them.

grass

A circle of grass that's
greener than the rest is
called a fairy ring.
Stand in the center, turn
three times, and make a wish.
If the fairy ring stays,
it can be wished on
once every three days.

halloween

On the day of Hallo-
ween, walk backward out
of your front door and
pick up some dust or grass.
Wrap it in paper and
put it under your pillow
that night. If you make a
wish before falling asleep,
it will come true.

hay wagon

Make a wish if you see a hay wagon, and say:

*"Load of hay,
load of hay,
Make a wish and
turn away."*

If you see the same hay wagon again, your wish *won't* come true.

WISCONSIN

horse

If you see a white horse,
make a wish, then look
around for a red-haired
woman. If you see one, your
wish will come true.

If you see a white horse
and don't cross your fingers
(or stamp your foot once),

and then make a wish,
you'll have bad luck.

If you see a black horse,
shake your fist at it three
times while making a wish.
If the horse looks at you,
there's a better chance
of the wish coming true.

If you see a gray horse,
spit first, then make a wish.

horseshoe

When you hang a horse-
shoe on a wall,
make a wish for good luck.

Hanging it with the ends
pointing up captures and holds
good luck; hanging it with
the ends pointing down allows
the luck to flow freely.

United States

ides, wishing

The "ides" of the ancient Roman calendar fell on the 15th days of March, May, July, and October, and on the 13th day of the other months.

Within one hour after midnight of an ides, and before speaking to anyone,

on a day of

cross your arms on your chest, touch
each shoulder with the opposite hand
and silently make a wish, repeating it in
your mind three times. Then nod your
head three times before taking your
arms out of the crossed position.

itching

If your ear itches, cover it
and make a wish that only good
will be spoken about you.

If your eye itches, don't rub it.
Cover it with one hand
as you wish for something or
someone you'd like to see.

If your nose itches, make a small
x on the tip and make a wish.

If your lips itch, press
them together and make a wish.

If the palm of your hand itches,
scratch it and say this chant
as you wish for money:
"Money itch, Money itch,
Money itch, Money come true."

If your foot itches, stamp it
three times and wish
to go to a certain place.

jockey

If you happen to see
a jockey who's wearing
his riding silks out-
side of the racetrack,
make a wish.

jug

When blowing
into a jug, if you
can get a sound
on the first try,
make a wish.

key

If you find a key that
someone else has lost,
make a wish before
picking it up. If you find
its owner, there's a
good chance that your
wish will come true.

knife

If you accidentally
drop a knife or
any other flatware,
make a wish before
you pick it up.